SUPER SANDCASTLE
It's the Alphabet!

It's X!

Katherine Hengel

Consulting Editor, Diane Craig, M.A./Reading Specialist

Published by ABDO Publishing Company, 8000 West 78th Street, Edina, Minnesota 55439. Copyright © 2010 by Abdo Consulting Group, Inc. International copyrights reserved in all countries. No part of this book may be reproduced in any form without written permission from the publisher. Super SandCastle™ is a trademark and logo of ABDO Publishing Company.

Printed in the United States.

 PRINTED ON RECYCLED PAPER

Editor: Liz Salzmann
Content Developer: Nancy Tuminelly
Cover and Interior Design and Production: Kelly Doudna, Mighty Media
Photo Credits: iStockphoto (Jani Bryson, Paul Kline), Shutterstock
Xerox® is a registered trademark of Xerox Corporation.

Library of Congress Cataloging-in-Publication Data
Hengel, Katherine.
  It's X! / Katherine Hengel.
    p. cm. -- (It's the alphabet!)
  ISBN 978-1-60453-611-9
  1. English language--Alphabet--Juvenile literature. 2. Alphabet books--Juvenile literature. I. Title.
  PE1155.H4688 2010
  421'.1--dc22
  〈E〉
                                    2009022182

JEASY
ITS

Super SandCastle™ books are created by a team of professional educators, reading specialists, and content developers around five essential components—phonemic awareness, phonics, vocabulary, text comprehension, and fluency—to assist young readers as they develop reading skills and strategies and increase their general knowledge. All books are written, reviewed, and leveled for guided reading, early reading intervention, and Accelerated Reader® programs for use in shared, guided, and independent reading and writing activities to support a balanced approach to literacy instruction.

About SUPER SANDCASTLE™

Bigger Books for Emerging Readers Grades K–4

Created for library, classroom, and at-home use, Super SandCastle™ books support and engage young readers as they develop and build literacy skills and will increase their general knowledge about the world around them. Super SandCastle™ books are an extension of SandCastle™, the leading preK–3 imprint for emerging and beginning readers. Super SandCastle™ features a larger trim size for more reading fun.

Let Us Know
Super SandCastle™ would like to hear your stories about reading this book. What was your favorite page? Was there something hard that you needed help with? Share the ups and downs of learning to read. We want to hear from you! Send us an e-mail.

sandcastle@abdopublishing.com

Contact us for a complete list of SandCastle™, Super SandCastle™, and other nonfiction and fiction titles from ABDO Publishing Company.

www.abdopublishing.com • 8000 West 78th Street
Edina, MN 55439 • 800-800-1312 • 952-831-1632 fax

Aa Bb Cc Dd Ee
Ff Gg Hh Ii Jj Kk
Ll Mm Nn Oo Pp
Qq Rr Ss Tt Uu Vv
Ww Xx Yy Zz

The Letter

The letter x in
American Sign Language

X and x can also look like

Xx **Xx** Xx Xx Xx Xx

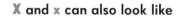

The letter x is a consonant.

It is the 24th letter of the alphabet.

Some words start with **x**.

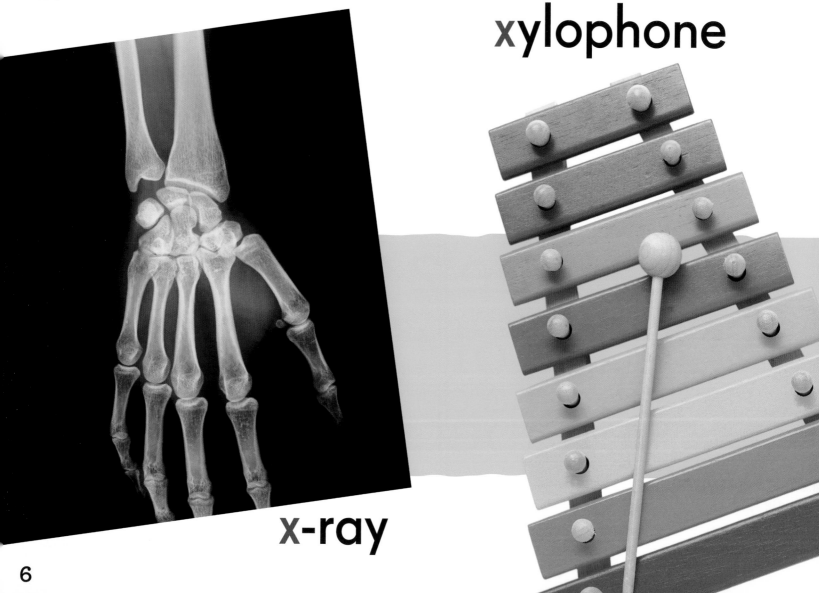

xylophone

x-ray

6

Xavier

Very few English words start with x.

Xavier likes to play the xylophone and look at x-rays.

Some words have **x** in the middle.

taxi

boxer

8

Alexis

It took Alexis sixteen hours
to drive her boxer
to Texas in a taxi.

Texas

Some words end with **x**.

fox

sax

10

Max

Max opened his mailbox and found a fox playing six songs on a sax.

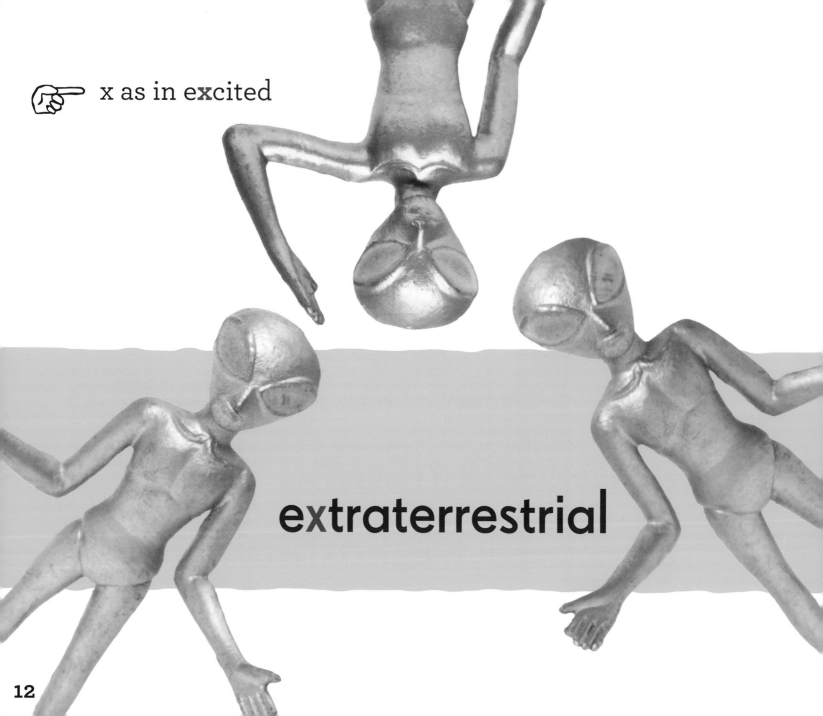

x as in e**x**cited

e**x**traterrestrial

Ms. Exley

Ms. Exley's class is excited about exploring the excellent extraterrestrial exhibit.

13

An ox named Rex lives in Texas.
He loves to explore.

His friend Trixie is a lynx
who lives right next door.

Rex and Trixie exercise
from two until six.

They always flex and
do sixty high kicks.

Then one day
a fox driving a taxi gives Rex a box.

Rex says, "There's been a mix-up.
This box is for Mr. Knox."

Deliver to: Mr. Knox
Fort Dix

17

Trixie exclaims, "How exciting! Here's a problem to fix."

Rex examines the box and says, "Mr. Knox lives in Fort Dix."

Trixie wants to send the box
to Fort Dix in a boxcar.

Rex says, "Let's just fax Mr. Knox
and explain where we are."

Mr. Knox
Exceptional Ibex
and
Xylophone Expert
Fort Dix, Extension 616

Sixteen days later, an ibex in a tux comes to Rex's home.

He says, "Excellent! I'm Mr. Knox, and you found my xylophone!"

Deliver to: Mr. Knox
Fort Dix

XYLOPHONEX
EXCELLENCE IN SHIPPING

21

Which words have
the letter **x**?

taxi

fox xylophone olive

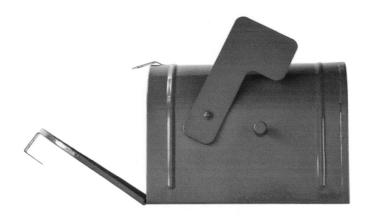

mailbox

book

apple

boxcar

Glossary

boxer (pp. 8, 9) – a medium-sized breed of dog.

examine (p. 18) – to look at closely.

extraterrestrial (pp. 12, 13) – a creature from outer space or another planet.

flex (p. 16) – to bend and stretch a muscle in the body.

ibex (p. 20) – a wild goat with large, curved horns.

sax (pp. 10, 11) – short for saxophone, a woodwind instrument that is made of metal.

tux (p. 20)– short for tuxedo, a man's formal suit that is worn with a white shirt and bow tie.

x-ray (pp. 6, 7) – a photograph of the inside of the body or another object.

xylophone (pp. 6, 7, 20, 22) – an instrument made of wooden or metal bars that you hit with wooden hammers.

To promote letter recognition, letters are highlighted instead of glossary words in this series. The page numbers above indicate where the glossary words can be found.

More Words with X

Find the **x** in the beginning, middle, or end of each word.

ax	exact	expect	mix	tax
axe	exam	expense	mixed	textbook
axis	example	experiment	mixture	toxic
axle	excuse	explode	oxygen	T. Rex
boxing	exist	galaxy	relax	wax
deluxe	exit	icebox	sixth	Xerox